THE ROAD TO GOWEL

Mary Guckian

For: Tim,
Enjoy the memories
Mary Guckian

Swan Press

Published by Swan Press,
32 Joy Street,
Dublin 4.

ISBN 0 9521342 8 4

Photographs by Mary Guckian

Back Cover: Photograph by Paul Wearen

Set by M Shine, Dublin

Dedicated to my sister Pauline Flynn,
who left us for her final home in May 1996.
Our time together growing up,
was full of life and joy.
Her loving, generous and warm personality
is remembered by all who knew her.

Acknowledgements

The Author is grateful to the following publications in which many of these poems first appeared:

Anglo-Celt, Artbeat, Asylum, Books Ireland, Brou Ha Ha, (USA), *Broad Seat,* (Australia), *Cerberus,* (USA), *Corran Herald, Extended Wings 1, 2, 4, Fine Line,* (Australia), *First Time, Free Xpression,* (Australia), *Hear My Song, Impact, Ingredients of Poetry, Inscriptions, Journeys of the Mind, Labour of Lov*e, (Canada), *Lateral Moves, Leitrim Observer, Library Association of Ireland Newsletter, Modern Woman, Peer Poetry, Perceptions, Quartet, Quantum Leap, Roscommon Herald, Rustic Rub, Sidewalk,* (Australia), *Studies, Tears in the Fence, Voices, ZZZ Zine,* (USA), *Centoria,* (Australia), *Towards the Millennium, Poetry Monthly, Riposte, Poets International*, (India), *Reflections, News Four.*

The Road to Gowel was broadcast on RTE Radio 1.

Many thanks to the Rathmines Writers' Workshop for their support and encouragement and thanks also to Mary Shine for her editorial assistance.

Contents

SANDYMOUNT STRAND

In the furrowed sand
puddles fill the hollow spaces,
the tide slowly overtakes the strollers,
wandering out into the vast expanse
of Sandymount Strand.

I recall the time we sat in the car
near Sligo -
tossing Atlantic waves bamboozling us,
the sea circling our space,
the car sinking in the sliding sand.

Working at our art, we take risks,
move out into wider horizons
and flourish,
but the surrounding tide is waiting
and swallows our masterpieces.

SNOW MORNING

For Pauline Flynn

I walk to work along Shelbourne Road,
after the Christmas holiday.
Inches of snow cover over the gardens;
on the trees each branch looks like a stroke
of artist's white paint,
and lilies laden with delicate meringues
form fairy designs.
Bunches of red fruit on the cotoneaster
give a warm glow to the cold day.
Hedges, stifled from constant trimming,
bear spheres of whiteness,
squashed into the tight branches;
the grass is covered in a cotton carpet,
and sleet drops mark out a pattern,
reminding me of the farm after a snowfall,
when the hens criss-crossed the garden
outside the kitchen window.

AT THE SITE

I trim the grass and trample the growth
around the trees we planted,
in the damp earth at Cloncolry.
You are carried away at owning a field
in the heart of a boggy landscape;
a place to read and write and gaze
at the animals, as they graze across fences.

I am used to working the soil and know
all about the hard labour of fighting nature.
I try to control the heavy growth that smothers
the new shrubs, on this one acre that nature
has endowed with moist clay,
where the profusion seems never ending.

Returning every few weeks,
I fight back with clippers.
A year later the hedges seem thinner,
the trees show their shapes
as I continue to flatten the growth around them,
ensuring that they breathe and grow
in the wildness of a Leitrim field.

Flooded river Shannon

Photograph by Mary Guckian

LONELY SHANNON WALK

You held my hand and led me
by the Shannon Walk,
among the reeds and spooky slopes
when the night was dark.
It was good to have you near,
feel your body close to mine,
as we walked hand in hand.
Your firm grip shielded me
from slipping on the shiny wood
into the lonely Shannon waters,
on a cold winter's night.
You steered me through the floods
and messy ground as we neared the end.
And then you held me close,
sharing a few of life's moments,
before we drifted away into nothingness,
like all of human creation
moving on its lonely course,
with moments of beauty
to keep us sane in between.

GLENVIEW HOTEL GARDENS, CO. WICKLOW

Down in the gardens
I walk among trees and flowers.
The colours are a revelation,
and every year I see more beauty
stretch before my eyes.
I wonder at the power of nature
and why I am here.

On the main road cars fly past,
as people return to the city
after the long week-end,
but in the midst of this enthralling
landscape, I think only of Pauline
and how she was taken from us
three weeks ago.

How she would have loved
this place of tall trees and birdsong.
Most of all, I remember the joy
she gave us, on each visit to her home
with Michael, at Kilmadderoe.

REMEMBERING COUNTESS MARKIEVICZ

Women politicians frame your bust
for the newspaper photographers
in St. Stephen's Green,
and remember your dream,
as they recall the pots of soup in Liberty Hall.
You planted flowers around
the tenements in Dublin,
and brought nature and beauty
to a revolutionary meeting,
as history was made
when they appointed you,
the first woman in the world,
as Minister for Labour.
Wearing tight corsets,
you rode through the fields
of your father's estate in County Sligo,
and saw how the tenants lived.
One of your last issues
was women's right to hold land.
The long years in prison,
where you painted water colours
and wrote poetry,
damaged your health,
but your last words sang:-
they are not dead, they do not sleep,
they have awakened from the dream of life.

KICKING STONES

In villages and towns around Ireland,
barefooted children played on the streets,
wearing garments that hung loosely,
too large for their hungry bodies.

Others worked in the mills and on farms,
or minded babies, with no toys for play,
only pieces of broken wood and stones
to kick about.

Behind high walls in the big houses,
the young were left in nurseries,
seldom seeing their parents,
who were often away in London
or visiting other country houses.

At home women made dolls' clothes
for their children,
while their husbands were away at war,
or shot pheasant and snipe on their estates.

In the evenings -
sumptuous meals were carried along
damp corridors by exhausted maids,
who worked hard to keep the food warm,
as many courses were laid on tables.

Later, the women retired
to their needle-work and gossip,
leaving the men to their battle talk,
their brandy and port,
while children remained safely out of sight.

THE LETTER

Your letter
I hold in my hand,
and read it over and over.
Absorbing your words,
I kiss the pages,
these pages your hands
have touched.
I see your pen move,
forming each word,
and feel a veil of love
encircling both of us,
though you are far away.
I go to sleep
keeping your letter
in my hands,
pressing it close
to my heart,
feeling your love tender
as an autumn sunset,
over Oxford's erect spires.

SCATTERED STONES ON THE BEACH

Stones -
all sizes, all shapes
scattered on the sands.
Stones like people drifting,
changing, loving,
in pieces, torn apart.
Others perfect -
rich colours, beautiful shapes.
On this beach
stones of every kind,
like people dispersed
to different corners of the globe.
All lie peaceful
every night, of every life,
no matter what society
may say or do.
Lucky stones.

CRUCIFIXION

Born with the image over our beds,
bombarded throughout our lives
with its presence,
in our schools and churches,
halls and hospitals,
galleries and museums;
haunted by a man hanging
from two pieces of wood.
A time may come for some of us,
to break free of the complexities
of our sexuality,
the pain of our damaged lives,
finally making the ultimate
sacrifice,
joining this sorrowful man.

PRINCESS DI

Like voyeurs we waited,
watched your movement
from a shy young girl,
to a mother full of courage,
sharing yourself with the world.
Now that you have left us,
we here, desperate, need
another face to focus on.

FLICKERING EMBERS

You expect me to sit beside you
just because you like to drink,
but I long to be on the dance floor,
moving to the music,
shaking to its every beat.

You are happy to sit drinking,
dreaming, as long as I am here too,
but I've had enough of waiting.
Sometimes - love cannot carry
all we want or need.

Right now
I'd rather be at home,
writing or painting in my flat.

HOLY JOE

Walking along the quays
on All Saints Day,
I watched the stooped old man,
partly hidden under a cap,
meticulously peel the posters
from the iron pillar box.
'Freedom for Women'
were the words I caught.
I wondered about him:
his feelings for his mother,
did he have a sister
or ever love a wife;
maybe he had a daughter?
The plastic bag he carried
was bulging with the paper,
he had spent the day removing
with his old worn hands.

OMAGH - August 15, 1998

Across the border for the first time,
on a Thursday, the Senior Citizens
travelled by coach to Omagh.
Driving over tidy roads, past the red
postal boxes and well-tilled fields,
they soaked in the Northern landscape.

The following Saturday, television
pictures showed crumbled buildings,
ambulance men carrying broken bodies,
many covered in burns and caked blood,
and every age group standing about in shock.

On Sunday the TV announcers
gave them the news: twenty-eight dead,
two hundred injured, most of them young.
Confused and frightened, the Senior Citizens
now need courage to cross the border,
be among people they know want peace.

ANTI-RACISM

Shadows on the wall displayed rabbits ears
from the folded hands of my father and mother
telling stories from the Far East
and African magazines.
They were magic to us then in the fifties.

We collected our pennies
to help the white-robed sisters and brothers,
care for the girls and boys with wondrous eyes,
who lived so far away.

The children of the children we admired,
now walk our city streets,
giving us a golden opportunity
to learn of other cultures,
experience their music, enjoy exotic foods,
new fabrics and designs.

We don't need to surf the Internet
in our sitting rooms,
to expand our horizons.

AUNTIE FAN

Yellow dandelions of yesterday,
all grey spores today,
you are no longer with us,
your spirit has flown away.

The lane bustles with people
reminiscing on your life.
Fields overflow with hayseed
shimmering in the breeze,
where bees are buzzing
and the birds sing.

You look beautiful laid out,
as we kneel and pray,
while your grand-children place
fresh flowers over your hands.

Later driving under tall ash trees
that crown the entrance to Creevagh,
we look across at the water lapping
the stony edge of the lake shore,
where Jack fished for pike during
the forty-seven years of your busy lives.

By the graveside we join together
to send you off to where we all must go.
You leave behind eleven children,
keeping your memory alive.

Milton Hebold sculpture of James Joyce at
Fluntern Cemetery, Zurich

Photograph by Mary Guckian

BLOOMSDAY
Reading at St Anne's Church, Dawson St

At the poetry reading
you are sensitive
to the unclear sounds,
the untrained voices.
Your ear never hears
the writer's words;
instead you become
edgy and agitated.
Before the first half
you are gone in search
of your own voice,
and never ending dreams.
I stay to listen,
absorb all the words,
follow the stories,
and feel inebriated
by this new writing.

Traditional music fills
the old Church,
here in Dawson St,
with flowing melodies.
A beat of feet balances
the sweetness of sound
with the way words,
placed in a new order,
lighten up our consciousness,
give meaning to our lives.
If only you would curb
your critical ear,
listen with your heart.

ESCAPING GENEVA

The Angelus bell rings in the village,
where the church has a trimmed edge
of fern trees, reminding me of the graveyard
at home, in Leitrim. The locked gate and
Alsatian dog, warn me not to venture inside.
In fields full of growth, wheat seeds thicken,
ridges drift across the valley
and disappear into the blue mountain,
that stands beneath a patterned sky,
where clouds roll towards the heavens.
I hear the sound of stones breaking
in the distance; a plane glides over my head,
I see one man caring for his vegetables
in a garden full of green heads and Chinese cabbage.
On the quiet road cyclists dressed in skin-fitted
luminous green and pink, fly past.
Birds never stop chirruping here,
where I could sit forever, never going
back to Geneva's working quarters.

NEGLECTED MUSE

Mind alert, the body tired,
thoughts take over,
words come thundering in.
The alarm set, I try to sleep,
but sounds won't go away.
I long to reach for paper,
a pen, but the body aches.
I think of work, the mortgage,
the post on my desk,
urgent letters in the dictaphone,
meetings to be organised,
minutes yet to be typed,
and wages at the week's end.
Words flow away on nights like these
and are never found again.

Meeting My Mother

My name is Mel. I was christened after the patron saint of the diocese where my mother lived. This is not unusual as I was born in a convent in a midland town and my mother was advised to call me after this saint. I would have liked a different name but my mother was thankful to have a place to stay while she waited to give birth. Ireland was a cold place in the forties and the year I was born in 1947, heavy snow came down and, even to this day, it was known as 'The Big Fall of '47'. My mother, whose name is Moya, was pregnant with me and I was born in July of that year and weighed almost 11lbs at birth. She was 18 years old.

The boy she had been in love with was called Phelim but tragically he died in a car accident on the way home from Dublin, from an All Ireland semi-final hurling match. It is Phelim's friend who is my father, his name is Jack and he consoled Moya after the accident. Phelim and Moya had been very much in love and Moya was devastated after his death but Jack was kind and comforting. Some weeks later they came to Dublin and stayed at a bed and breakfast in Gardiner St., not far from Croke Park. It was there I was conceived. Jack found it difficult to cope with the pregnancy and a few months later he emigrated to England leaving Moya to fend for herself.

Families were intolerant of pregnancies outside of marriage at that time. After finding the courage to tell her parents she was pregnant they told her she would burn in hell for her sin. In fear she went to confession and met a kind priest who told her about a place she could stay for the remainder of her pregnancy. She told him that she would be better off dead than having to go on living at home. The neighbours had made her feel dirty and not fit to live among them. The priest arranged for Moya to be admitted to the convent in the midlands and she arrived just before the big fall of snow in May. She had one change of clothes, a few shillings to cover her bus fare to Dublin and from there to the midland town where the only souvenir she had with her was a photograph of Phelim, who she had loved, but none of my father. This made me sad when she told me her story twenty-seven years later. Moya had tears in her eyes as she recalled what had happened to her. Her parents never said goodbye and the journey was frightening as she had no idea what kind of a place, was going to become her home for the next few months.

On her arrival a nun with a worn and worried look in her face led her into a large room, which she was to share with ten other pregnant girls. The building was cold and bleak with whitewashed walls and dark iron beds, covered in icy white quilts. Outside the snow came down in large gentle petals and, despite the bareness, a certain peace emanated from this place where she would bring me into the world. Moya was given some hot cocoa, home made brown bread and butter, followed by bread and butter pudding. Some of the nuns liked to cook but the food was scarce and she was often hungry. She missed the boiled potatoes, which had been plentiful on the farm, and the milk she had drunk whenever she was thirsty. All she had was the grey water from the tap in the big, old, stone-floored kitchen. A lot of Moya's time was spent scrubbing the old stairs that led to the room on the first floor where all the girls lay down at night. With the ringing of a bell by an old man at 5.30 a.m. the girls had to get up and attend morning Mass at 6 a.m. Morning sickness was not tolerated and it was important to thank God for giving them a place to stay while waiting for their babies.

Moya liked sewing and she had the job of repairing the heavy old curtains. As she was anxious to make clothes for the new baby she used the left over pieces of material to make baby garments. After I was born she could not use them as babies wore a uniform that consisted of a tiny vest with a narrow ribbon that was tied around our bodies. A binder, eight inches wide, about a yard long, was wrapped around our tummies. This was supposed to give support to a new baby's back and it was held together with a large safety pin. A thin slip was put over our heads and a long white dress, buttoned at the back, went over this. The end of the material was wrapped around our feet so as to keep us cosy and warm in the cradle. The nappies were made of heavy, bulky material and we were all dressed in similar outfits and no distinction made between baby girls and boys.

I had to live with the stigma of illegitimacy when I found out the circumstances of my birth at sixteen years of age. The truth came as an enormous shock when I went along to purchase a birth certificate for my first job. There was no Dad on my certificate and my mother's name was different to the family I was living with. The Government have since changed my status and I can now get a Civil Service pension and share in any property my real father and mother may leave behind. I suffered much on several occasions when I went along for interviews and eyes would be raised to heaven when the employer looked at my birth certificate. My status changed immediately in their eyes despite how healthy I looked and well spoken I was.

I never blamed Katie or Paddy, my adopted parents. They did their best to give me as normal a life as they could and my adopted brothers and sisters were always kind to me, but I felt different. I was easy-going, very dark and broad shouldered. They were slightly built, lively, full of action and good at games. I hated games and wanted to read books. Reading was a sign of laziness in most families then so I tried to fit in and joined in sport, and rarely got an opportunity to read. Working on the farm and taking in what was happening around me, occupied a lot of time after school.

After spending much time in the Custom House searching for my mother's Birth Certificate, I eventually traced her. It took many trips, as I had to search for everyone with her name between the ages of sixteen and forty-five. I was glad I persevered as I got to know Moya. She has a very philosophic way of looking at life. I was lucky that I inherited the same spirit; otherwise, I might never have survived the shock of finding out that I was illegitimate.

Moya has told me she suffered much that time in 1947 when there was no income or no help for single parents. The nuns told Moya an advertisement would appear in the local paper to have me adopted and that is how I came to live in Cork. I was with her for six weeks after I was born. She told me that I was the most wonderful baby in the whole world, and rarely cried. The day I was taken from her was the saddest day she ever experienced.

Moya never lost her interest in clothes and makes her own and she always looks elegant when I meet her twice a year. That is our arrangement now as I live in Cork and she is married to a farmer near the border in Monaghan. She has one other son who is my blood brother and I now feel part of two families.

Away From Home

I grew up on a small farm where life was busy and at times exhausting, with cycling to school, doing my lessons, collecting food from the local store, helping out with my six younger sisters and brothers. Time flew and my teenage years passed rapidly. At seventeen, I went to work in a town 35 miles from home.

It was here I began to have more time for myself as the official working day finished at 5.30 pm. After eating my dinner, cooked in the digs, I began to get involved in local events that were open to outsiders. Most of my working colleagues were in the Legion of Mary so it was natural that I should join when lobbied by them. A meeting took place one evening each week, and another was spent visiting the sick at the local psychiatric hospital and the County Home for old people who were bed-ridden. Many of the patients did not have visitors and therefore were delighted with the company. I also learned First Aid at Civil Defence and attended craft classes in embroidery and tapestry.

Before long I also began to attend the local dances that were held on Friday nights. I had no idea about dancing but having moved into a flat, the girls I shared with, gave me some lessons on how to move around the floor without tripping my partner, or standing on his toes. On my first trip to the local dance hall, I discovered I had to overcome the hurdle of standing in the cold hall, waiting to be asked to dance. This took a lot of getting use to, for up to then, work consumed my life and I never knew what it was like to stand around and wait. Every minute of my time had been occupied, whether it was using a few free minutes to take up my knitting, or making garments for myself and my family, and even for my cousins, of which there were plenty, all younger than myself. Even after I left home, I was never idle in my spare time, as I continued to make my own clothes, having purchased a sewing machine with savings from my first few pay packets.

The waiting situation was made worse by the fact that in order to get a seat on the bus, I had to go before 9.30 pm, which meant I was at the hall very early. The band spent about an hour preparing the sound and the microphones, and many of the men only arrived after they had spent some time in the local pubs. Standing around waiting was certainly a huge culture shock and all sorts of thoughts went through my head. What if I didn't get asked to dance? How would I respond if someone did ask me?

These dances, however, soon became a part of my life and I began to enjoy hearing different showbands play, and listening to the words of their songs. At the end of the working week I looked forward to hearing *The Capital Showband, The Royal Blues, The Melody Aces, The Drifters, The Miami Showband,* and *The High Lows.*

Listening to the music was satisfying, and even if men were scarce, as many had emigrated in the fifties and early sixties to England, it was the songs and the tunes that made life pleasant. Reared without a radio until I was thirteen, I heard little music before then. Bridie Gallagher and Ruby Murray were two women I heard sing on the sponsored programmes when I was at home; one of their most popular tunes was *The Boys from the County Armagh.* Sometimes in the evening my father might sing *Three Lovely Lassies from Bannion and I am the Best of Them All,* or *The Old Bog Road.* Once he picked up a leaflet at a fair with the words of *The Croppy Boy* and *The Wild Colonial Boy.* We did have a gramophone at home, which was taken out a few times a year. Tune's like *The Stack O Barley* were played from the records, which came from America, through my Uncle Willie. John McCormack was there also. The other place I listened to singing was at the Church, at Sunday Benediction, where people sang such hymns as *Tantum Ergo, Faith of Our Fathers*, and *We Stand for God and for His Glory,* very enthusiastically. *The Leitrim Observer* regularly printed the words of songs, and I enjoyed reading them, and cutting out the words for pasting in my old copybooks.

The dances were becoming a real treat. Time passed quickly getting ready for my nights out. My hair had to be washed and rollers put in to keep the perm in place for a few weeks longer. The rollers, along with hairgrips, make-up and other necessary toiletries were bought at Woolworth's. It was a great shop for trimmings for dresses; knitting needles and patterns could also be got there. My perfume was either *Lily of the Valley* or *Apple Blossom.*

I usually met some fellow at the dance and some even asked to see me again. As the Fridays passed I got to know some who were good dancers while others were a bit awkward, but my steps improved and I began to move well to the music. By the time I was eighteen, a man a few years older, and well dressed with dark good looks, asked if he could take me to the local cinema, to a film starring John Wayne. Not having been to the cinema before, I was delighted with the prospect of this new experience and arranged to meet him a few days later.

Eventually the day arrived and I was full of excitement, with butterflies in my stomach and wondered how I would get on with this new man, Colm. I knew very little about him but went to a lot of trouble getting ready to meet him. My flatmates helped put in the rollers and advised me on what I should wear, but I chose what I felt most comfortable in. Examining myself in the mirror I could see that the new roll-on gave a shapely cut to my figure. These had become fashionable and were a lot more comfortable than corsets, as there were no steels boring into the rolls of skin around my waist. Finally the girls sprayed me with perfume and I put some vaseline on my patent shoes. I was ready for my night at the cinema.

I waited impatiently for Colm to collect me, with my lipstick blotted and the powder dabbed on my cheeks. But the time went on and Colm never appeared. For the first hour I thought he might have been held up at work, as he worked in a local bar, or he might be ill, but I never thought he would not show up. The long wait made my body wilt, the tight roll-on became a nuisance and my cheeks lost their glow. The night finally ended in the company of my flatmates. They tuned into the radio and started to dance, to cheer me up, and so the night passed. There were no phones in flats then and no way a message could be passed on.

The next morning I felt sad when I woke up. I headed into work and later in the day one of my friends, who as it happened was also a friend of Colm's sister, phoned to ask me why I had let Colm down. We eventually figured it out - he had gone to the wrong address! There was an Upper and a Lower Market Street. I didn't know whether to laugh or cry, but in a way I felt relieved, because at least he had not let me down. I had given him too little information. It was definitely a learning process. Next time I gave an address, I'd make sure I gave all the details.

Bicycle of Pilgrim from Poland parked along the wall of the Church of the Annunciation in Nazareth, September 2000.

Photograph by Mary Guckian

The Silenced Priest

The man that cycled by our home, in neat clerical garb and a round black hat, was quiet and inoffensive. He liked to visit the local town from time to time. People spoke in whispers about his healing powers and it was known that many people from all over Ireland came to visit him for cures.

In order to prevent the parishioners attending his Mass, it had to be celebrated at 6.30 a.m. in the morning. A few brave souls walked some miles to join him on Sunday mornings and then waited for the official priest to come and say Mass at the normal time of 8 o'clock.

In the evenings after school we watched for the number plates of cars when drivers looked for directions to the place where this man lived. Later from our Atlas we counted the number of miles they might have travelled. It was a treat to see new models of cars, as there was only the one model where we lived.

My mother cycled to visit him with offerings when my father was in hospital with pleurisy. I was ten years old and the six of us would wait for her return. We had a great belief in the power of this man and that he would help Daddy, ensuring that he would soon be back home with us.

This silenced priest was our saviour in the 1940s and 50s and we often wondered why he was expected to stay silent, as we believed that he was not allowed to speak. His spiritual powers were beyond our understanding but a comfort when trouble came round. We believed he was nearer to God and would help us when sickness and other problems occurred.

NIGHT TIME

The paraffin oil lamp glimmers,
shadows appear on the wall from the open fire,

smoke puffs back down from the chimney,
and fresh ash logs sizzle as they burn.

Chairs line in a circle before the fire,
as we children run around the floor,

playing house under the small table,
or making a Church in another corner,

giving out communion, going to confession.
We fight over cardboard boxes and build

shelves for a shop with empty tea packets,
Bird's jelly de-luxe and custard powder,

Bachelor's peas, all patched together.
Empty sacks lay across the door-end

to keep out the sharp breeze in winter.
Before bedtime we go outside to do a *shannon.*

Stars shine brightly in the sky on frosty nights,
and the moon pours light onto our bodies,

while dark shadows move in front of us,
scaring us in case some stranger is about.

We light a candle to take us upstairs to sleep,
our breath shaking the flame as we hurry on up.

The sheets are cold and shining white
but we warm up together, sleeping three to a bed.

We say our prayers: 'Matthew, Mark, Luke and John,
God bless the bed we lie on.'

In our imagination we can see the four saints,
one on each brass knob of the large iron bed.

SETTING THE POTATOES

We scored the earth
before digging sods with the loy,
to make ridges for setting potatoes
in the Spring.

We filled the cart with manure
from the pit
at the back of the cow byre.

Then we led the horse to the field,
where my father
unloaded fresh cow dung in a line
on each ridge.

We carried out the potato slits
that my mother cut,
making sure the growth of an eye
was left on each piece.

We placed them on the space
between the turned up sod
and the earth,
and then shovelled clay on top.

The clay was damp and dauby
on our skin,
slippery beneath our feet.

THE CINDER PASS

We loved to walk on the cinder path,
push the burned-out coals into the earth.

My father had shovelled the cinders
from the heap at the creamery,

after he had spilled the fresh milk
into big vats.

The cinders were heaved off the cart
at the back of the garden field

that led to the Square Meadow,
and on to Kilmadderoe Lake,

where the cattle plunged in
to keep cool in summer time.

In the winter time
the cinders created a dry walk,

when the fields were wet and mucky.
We helped to shape the path,

as we pounded on the soft stones,
crunching them back into the clay,

recycling the remains
from Kiltoghert Co-op.

SLAPS

My education was learning to write
in copy books and jotters,
trying to gain knowledge
to face the world,
and cope with its calamities.

I never learned much
and cried a lot of the time,
as daily the master took out the rod.
I listened to its whine
as it came down on each hand
so many times.
I was unable to count the slaps.

I watched so many suffer in silence.
They never shed a tear,
just held their hands limply,
and tried to bear the pain inflicted
by a man who was unaware.

He was afraid to touch me.
I cried for all the others,
my tears making blobs of blue ink
on each page of my copy book.
The scars are still livid,
like piercing nails under bare feet.

WINTER

I slowly come to life
walking by the canal bank,
absorbing the sounds of water,
the tingling of reeds in the breeze.
The fresh air prepares me
for a tedious day ahead,
behind a desk, typing, filing,
keeping the bosses happy,
and customers content.

View from Carrowkeel looking on to Lough Arrow, Co. Sligo.

Photograph by Mary Guckian

THE ROAD TO GOWEL

In winter we skidded on the frosted potholes,
to reach Gowel Church for the ceremonies

we faithfully attended. As the year moved on
we watched the gardens grow and climbing roses

frame the porches of the houses.
Thatchers patterned the roofs with saffron straw.

Smells of fresh manure speckled the road,
as farmers carted it away to spread upon the ridges,

before they ploughed the shapely furrows scored
with loys. We smelled the new mown grass

and watched the cocks of hay appear like domes
across the fields. With wisps of hay the twister shaped

the ropes that tied them firm, to keep the blustering
wind at bay, when showers came down.

The bluestone spray sprinkled the stalks of potato fields,
to keep the deadly blight away; stories of the famine

still haunted the memories of older people.
Going to confession on Saturdays, we met the carts,

some pulled by donkeys, some by horses.
Musical echoes filled our ears as cans were lifted

from outside the houses, and taken to the creamery.
Coming home again, we smelled skim milk taken back

to feed pigs, as it spilled from overflowing cans.
Sods of turf lay scattered on the road, fallen from crates

loaded on carts, coming from the bog.
Autumn came and fields were golden with oat seeds

swishing in the breeze. Women, bent in two,
gathered sheaves and tied them with blades of corn

from swarths left lying by the scythe. Later they looked
like mustard standing stones as stooks were made.

Dark grey days came round and men dug ridges,
the soil looked damp and dauby. Pink and white

potatoes lay in bunches on the cold clay, picked
by children when they came in from school.

Clamps were made secure to last the winter.
Christmas morning was the darkest, as fasting from

midnight, we left our houses to walk the road to Mass,
greeting our neighbours with happy Christmas,

along the way. We loved to look into the crib
and see the Holy family, among the animals,

sitting on the straw. Our whole year was circled
by this simple story of the newborn child.

SWALLOWS

Long tailed swallows
glided onto our street in springtime.

Their swift movements shaded our faces,
as they made for the barn, where their
nest clung to rafters under the roof.

They replenished the inside
of the speckled nest with wisps of hay,
and eggs were laid.

We longed for the babies to appear,
and watch them learn to fly,
before they journeyed south.

MISTY DAYS

The light changes quickly
as mist rains on the fields
where cattle shelter.

Heavy drops split,
as they hit the backs
of the coloured animals,
shading their coats.

Ducks quack at the pool edge,
leaving prints of webbed feet
in mushy soil.

The dog wanders
through the kitchen
shaking water
from his shaggy coat.

Children run along the road,
trying to stop the mist,
settling on their tiny faces.

A cart creaks by,
hitting puddles on the road.
The harness sheds water
onto the horse's body.

THE ORCHARD

Apple trees filled the back garden,
where we knew the shape of each tree,
picking the fallen apples when in season.
In late April and early May we played
under the blossoms and delicate petals
fell on us from a pink batik sky.

My mother made apple tarts from the large,
sour variety, baked on the open hearth,
the overflowing juice sizzling and burning
to a hard paste at the edge of the pan.
Returning from snigging in the cocks of hay,
or packing the saved meadows into the hayshed,
we devoured the sweet taste of apple-pie.

At Halloween a large apple hung
from the ceiling in our kitchen,
and with our hands tied behind our backs,
we strained to bite into its swinging shape,
much too big for our small mouths;
or we dived into a basin of water
getting drenched as we struggled to grip
the apple's hard green skin.

The remainder were stored in heaps,
and covered with rushes at the end of the garden.
These were used at Christmas when apple crumble
was baked in the oven under the rich, red coals,
placed on top of the lid, hanging
over the open hearth of the fireplace.

At St. Lasair's Well, Kilronan, Keadue, Co. Roscommon.

Photograph by Mary Guckian

THE ROSARY

The ash logs blazed behind us,
as we knelt down to the family rosary
on the cement hearth floor.
One prayer stays with me still:-

Angel of God, my guardian dear,
to whom God's love commits me here,
ever this night be at my side,
to light and guard, to rule and guide

The climb upstairs to bed afterwards,
was made easier as we watched
the dark shadows jump off the wall
from the shimmering candle light.

LITTLE CHRISTMAS

The excitement of seeing new faces
visit our small farm was over,

as relations and neighbours stopped calling.
I felt lonesome for the red-berried holly

and the crib packed away with the brass
candlesticks; the cosy atmosphere

of coloured crepe paper decorations,
cards and posters depicting *Merry Christmas,*

and *Happy New Year,* placed in old shoe boxes.
Letters that came with parcels from America

were put aside for acknowledgement.
Waiting for another twelve months

for Christmas cake, plum pudding
and the extra groceries from Murray's shop,

and the local Co-op, made time seem infinite.

LOWER DECK - 2000

Pubs change hands for millions of pounds,
then are torn asunder,
while skips are filled with well-worn wood,
old walls and lime dust,
blowing litter all over the city.

Upper decks are turned into restaurants
where golden wood covers the floors,
as eating out becomes our national pastime,
keeping our designer kitchens clean.

At the Lower Deck familiar faces
are there from week to week,
and the sound swells with old songs
from a different era.

EXCHANGE BUILDINGS

My working days in Dublin,
began at Exchange Buildings,
in the old part of the city.
Leslie, sitting at the grey entrance,
kept an eye on our movements,
as we skimmed past him when we left
a minute early for lunch,
or avoided his knowing eye whenever
we came back late.
I sat all day in a tiny space,
in the grim office,
responding to three hundred
extensions on the switchboard
and the thirty outgoing lines.
The only disturbance came
from the young insurance agents,
parking in the lane outside,
who tried to sell us insurance policies,
that gave young women
a lump sum when they married.

DART

As on each evening of the working week,
people surge forward,

climbing the steps to catch the Dart.
The carriages are soon crowded,

paper headlines prominently display
our latest tragedy; briefcases open

in the confined space, their owners
lose themselves in foolscap sheets.

Others yawn or doze fitfully,
heads lolling sideways as straight seats

refuse to give comfort, knees rub
against one's facing passenger.

Suffocating in an airless carriage,
as I reach upwards to open a window,

passengers stare at me in silence.

IN THE LIBRARY

Every morning they ask me
'Did you do the back-up?'
And every time I hear the words,
back-up, the street at home
floats before my eyes,
my father tackling the horse,
moving him under the shafts
of the cart, coaxing him,
back-up, back-up.

SIEVING THE SOIL

Escaping from my computer,
at the turn of the Victorian stairs,
the window fills with movement.

Like a dinosaur pounding the earth,
the large prongs of the digger, shift
the stones from the mounds of clay.

The temporary buildings were wiped out
in one day, to make room
for the Barrington-O'Reilly Hall.

The lair where the fox emerged,
with its red fur, is now flattened,
brightening our evenings no more,

and the trees rooted out, as the earth
is sieved and shaken, getting soil ready
for the new Millennium Garden.

Crane working over the Millennium Tower at
Charlotte Quay, Ringsend.

Photograph by Mary Guckian

THE CRANE DRIVER

You sit all day,
overlooking the city,
with bended knees in a tiny space,
where you guide connections,
moving the clear box
in different directions,
over high-rise buildings.

Viewing the city from this height
your eyes must tire,
as you scan the office blocks,
the factories and busy roads,
as thousands move in the city
from place to place.

Surrounded by Church spires,
how do you mange to sit
in the same spot
and keep the flow of movement
on the building site,
without getting dizzy?

You never seem to leave
and I wonder are you comfortable
so near the sky,
or do you feel claustrophobic,
locked in a box
for ten hours a day?

AMIENS STREET STATION

The grey tones of the new lobby,
at Amiens St Station,
shimmer on this hot July morning,
while the floor entrance to the café,
wet with spillages from cartons,
carried out by rush hour workers,
is wiped clean by Asian workers.

THE SLEEPER

You sleep on the far side
of the room, snoring,
to please your dreams.

Are they frightening tonight,
as you lie there,
unable to see your way out.

Stretched on your back,
the sounds become louder
from your bed,

but I am happy you are here,
no fear comes into my head.

HERBERT PARK

A cacophony of sound throbs through the park,
invading my lunch hour,
as the noise of planes soaring across the skyline,
mingles with the constant din of cars.

Sycamore trees surround the artificial lake,
and glop over the water's edge,
their branches battering against the cement path.

People throw bread into the lake
and ducks compete with water hens,
for a few crusts floating on the dark surface.

I watch as children delight in the movements
of young ducks as they follow the female,
until they are ready to fend for themselves,
along with other fowl in Herbert Park